David Harrison

The Melancholy Narrative of the Distressful Voyage and Miraculous Deliverance

of Captain David Harrison of the sloop, Peggy, of New-York, on his voyage

from Fyal, one of the Western Islands, to New-York

David Harrison

The Melancholy Narrative of the Distressful Voyage and Miraculous Deliverance
*of Captain David Harrison of the sloop, Peggy, of New-York, on his voyage from
Fyal, one of the Western Islands, to New-York*

ISBN/EAN: 9783337091880

Printed in Europe, USA, Canada, Australia, Japan

Cover: Foto ©Andreas Hilbeck / pixelio.de

More available books at **www.hansebooks.com**

THE
MELANCHOLY NARRATIVE

OF THE

DISTRESSFUL VOYAGE

AND

MIRACULOUS DELIVERANCE

OF

Captain *David Harrifon*,

OF THE

SLOOP, *PEGGY*,

OF

NEW-YORK, on his Voyage from FYAL, one
of the Weftern Iflands, to NEW-YORK,

WHO

Having loft all his Sails in a long Series of hard Weather, and
entirely exhaufted his Provifions, lived two and forty Days
without receiving the leaft Food, till he was happily
relieved by the Humanity of Capt. EVERS of the *Sufanna*,
in the *Virginia* Trade.—In this Narrative the Expedients
which Capt. HARRISON and his Men made Ufe of
for their Subfiftence are particularly fet forth, who twice
caft Lots for their Lives, and were to have killed the
fecond Man on the very Morning they were providen-
tially taken up,—The Whole being authenticated in the
ftrongeft Manner, by repeated Depofitions,

BEFORE THE

Right Hon. *GEORGE NELSON*, Efq.
Lord-Mayor of the City of LONDON,

AND

Mr. *ROBERT SHANK*, Notary Public.

WRITTEN BY HIMSELF.

LONDON,

Printed for JAMES HARRISON, oppofite STATIONERS'
HALL, LUDGATE-STREET.

M DCC LXVI.

THE

MELANCHOLY NARRATIVE

OF THE

DISTRESSFUL VOYAGE

AND

MIRACULOUS DELIVERANCE

OF

Captain *David Harrison.*

THE occurrences of my late unfortunate voyage, are of a nature so extraordinary, and my preservation is a circumstance so miraculous, that, sensible as I am at present of the Divine goodness, it would look like a want of gratitude to the great disposer of all things, if I neglected to employ a few hours in the recital of some particulars, where his Providence has been singularly

B   manifested,

manifefted, and where he has given an inconteftible leffon to all his creatures, to dread the impiety of defpair, fince his affiftance may be neareft at hand when they are leaft in expectation of relief.

THE folemnity of this fentiment will not, I hope, terrify a reader of elegance from the perufal of the following pages. — Thofe who read for mere amufement, will probably find fomething to entertain them, unlefs they are too refined to put up in real diftrefs with thofe circumftances which would poffibly yield them moft fatisfaction in a work of mere imagination, — while thofe who are actuated by a more ferious turn, will poffibly exclaim in the exalted language of the Pfalmift, " How wonderful are the works of the " Lord, how great in wifdom all."

WITHOUT farther preface, I weighed anchor at NEW-YORK, on the 25th of Auguft,

Auguft, 1765, and came to fail from SANDY HOOK on the 27th with a cargo confifting of lumber, ftaves, bees-wax, fifh, &c. and proceeded on my intended voyage, with a fmall breeze of wind, at S. S. W. — Nothing remarkable occurred on the outward bound part of my paffage, and arrived fafe at FYAL on the 5th of October following—where I immediately addreffed myfelf to the Britifh conful at that place, Mr. Richard Gathorne, and his partner, Mr. Alexander Graham, purfuant to my inftructions, and after clearing my fhip in the cuftomary mercantile courfe, I got a cargo of wine, brandy, &c. for NEW-YORK, by the 22d of October, which I had no fooner completed, than I went immediately on fhore for my letters and difpatches; apprehenfive of the confequences of coming on the coaft of AMERICA, in a fingle deck veffel, in the winter feafon, a time in which thefe feas are uncommonly dangerous.

EVERY

EVERY thing being ready by the 24th, — I fet fail about half after eleven in the morning from FYAL, with a fine breeze of wind at S. E. and at fix o'clock in the evening the body of the ifland bearing from me North, three leagues, I loft fight of land, and began to flatter myfelf with the hopes of a very expeditious voyage. On the 29th, however matters put on quite a different afpect ; the wind blowing pretty frefh, my ftanding jib, a very old one indeed, was fplit, and as we had no other on board, we unbent and put it into as good a condition as the nature of our cir-cumftances would admit. — The violence of the weather ftill continuing, we went under an eafy fail, a double-reefed main-fail and jib. — Neverthelefs on Wednefday the 6th of November, two pair of my foremoft main-fhrouds, on the larboard fide, were carried away, being old and unable to refift the feverity of the weather. — On this we immediately fet

up

up ſtoppers; and got a runner and tackle as a ſupport to the maſt; lying too under a ballanced mainſail, as it blew extremely hard. — The next day the wind ſhifting to the W. N. W. and blowing more violently, we wore ſhip, and laid her head to the Southward; but about eight o'clock in the morning, my two fore main ſhrouds, on the ſtarboard ſide, were carried away, which obliged us to get up another runner and tackle for the additional ſecurity of the maſt. — ' Till the 12th of November, the weather was intolerably bad, the ſeas exceſſively heavy, and the continued peals of thunder joined to our incapacity of carrying any ſail, unleſs for a few hours, threw a horror over our ſituation, which is not to be conceived by any but thoſe who have unhappily experienced ſomething like our circumſtances.

On Tueſday, the 12th of November, the weather ſeemed more moderate, though the

the change did not carry the appearance of any great duration; and, indeed, next day, to our unfpeakable mortification, it came on to blow as hard as ever at W. N. W. fo that my fore-ftay and fore-fheets were not only torn away, but the fore-fail itfelf rent in pieces ; and what added confiderably to the lofs, was my not having any other to put in it's place.—In this fituation we lay too, as before, under a ballanced reefed main-fail, the impetuofity of the ftorm ftill continuing, and the feas rolling mountains high, all of us expecting that the veffel would prove leaky, as fhe ftrained inconceivably hard.

SCUDDING away, however, on the 16th or 17th, under the fquare fail head, about two in the morning, the tack unfortunately happening to give way, this fail was torn all to tatters, fo that we were obliged to cut it from the yard, and to heave too immediately under bare poles till the main-

fail

fail was ballanced reefed.—One misfortune is generally the forerunner of another ; at leaft we found it fo; for while we lay too in the fame gale of wind, which deftroyed our fquare fail, the flying jib blew overboard, from a new fet of points, although it was a new fail, and made of top-gallant duck. — Notwithftanding all thefe accidents, we made fome little way, at intervals, under an eafy fail, till the 1ft of December, when being attacked by another violent gale, in the latitude of 40 d. 1 m. North, and longitude 58 d. 37 m. Weft from LONDON, a dreadful fea broke two of my main chain-plates, and fhattered my fore-fail to fuch a degree, as rendered it utterly unferviceable. — The only bit of canvafs now left, was the main-fail, which we backed and lay too, having no profpect whatever before us but what was pregnant with the bittereft diftrefs ; for the conflict which our veffel had fo long

maintained

maintained againſt waves and winds, had, by this time, occaſioned her to leak exceſſively; and our proviſions were ſo much exhauſted, that we found it abſolutely neceſſary to come to an immediate allowance of two pounds of bread a week, for each perſon, beſides a quart of water, and a pint of wine a day. — The alternative was really deplorable, between the ſhortneſs of our proviſions, and the wreck of our ſhip. If we contrived to keep the latter from ſinking, we were in danger of periſhing with hunger, and if we contrived to ſpin out the former with a rigid perſeverance of œconomy for any time, there was but little probability of being able to preſerve our ſhip, — thus, on either hand, little leſs than a miracle could ſave us from inevitable deſtruction; if we had an accidental gleam of comfort on one hand, the fate with which the other ſo viſibly teemed, gave an inſtant check to our ſatisfaction, and obſcured every

rifing

riſing ray of hope, with an inſtant cloud
of horror and deſpair.

WE met, indeed, a couple of veſſels,
one from JAMAICA for LONDON, and
another to DUBLIN, from NEW-YORK,
who would have probably relieved us,
had there been a poſſibility in ſo ſevere
a gale, to open any cummunication from
ſhip to ſhip ; all they could do was to
ſpeak to us, a circumſtance which the
reader's own imagination muſt naturally
ſuppoſe did not a little add to the miſery
of our ſituation. — Diſappointed of ſuc-
cour in this quarter, I was under a neceſſity of contracting the little allowance
which had been lately ſettled for each
man ; and continued gradually leſſening
the quantity of proviſions, till every
morſel was entirely exhauſted, and not
above two gallons of dirty water remaining in the bottom of a caſk. My
poor fellows, who from inceſſant fatigue,
and a long want of neceſſaries, were now

reduced

reduced to a very weakly condition, began at laſt to grow impatient, and ſeized on the cargo, naturally enough obſerving that the wine and brandy were the only things they had now remaining in the world; and that I muſt not be ſurprized if they made very free with both, for their ſupport. — I could neither be ſorry nor ſurprized at this motion. — What gave me concern was, the continual exceſs to which they drank — and the continual courſe of execration and blaſphemy, which was occaſioned by that exceſs. — For my own part, I abſtained, as much as poſſible, from wine, and very gladly huſbanded the dregs of the water caſk, which afterwards proved of infinite ſervice to me, and may be not improperly reckoned an eſſential means of my ſurviving a complication of the moſt affecting calamities.

OUR veſſel had been for ſome time toſſed about, at the mercy of the winds and

and waves, when in the midſt of our
deſpair, we were ſuddenly tranſported
with the moſt extravagant ſenſations
of joy, by the diſcovery of a ſail to the
leeward, the 25th of December, in the
morning. — Diſtreſs generally inſpires
the human mind with lively ſentiments
of devotion, and thoſe, who, perhaps,
diſpute or diſregard the exiſtence of a
Deity at other times, are ready enough,
in the day of adverſity, to think every
advantageous turn in their affairs a particular exertion of the Divine benignity.—
It was, therefore, but natural for ſome
of the people to think that the 25th of
December was appointed for their preſervation, in a temporal ſenſe, as much
as in a ſpiritual view it was appointed
to be the means of their future felicity.
— Our thankſgivings, however, to Providence, though profoundly ſincere, were
not offered in any great form. We all
crouded upon deck; and hung out, with
our utmoſt expedition, a proper ſignal of

diſtreſs;

diftrefs; and, about eleven o'clock, had
the unfpeakable fatisfaction, to come near
enough to the fhip to engage her in conver-
fation, to inform her of our diftreffes; and
to obtain from the captain an affurance
of relief. — Indeed the promifed relief
was but fmall, neverthelefs, the fmalleft
to people in our circumftances, was in-
eftimable. It was to be nothing more
than a little bread, which was all, as the
captain affured me, that he could fpare,
as he himfelf was contracted in every
other article. — This, however, he faid
we fhould have, as foon as he had
finifhed an obfervation which he was
taking, for it was now near twelve
o'clock. — Having no doubt, in nature,
but the captain would punctually perform
his promife, I retired to reft myfelf in
the cabbin, being much emaciated with
fafting and fatigue; and labouring, at the
fame time, not only under a very dreadful flux, but a fevere rheumatifm in my
right knee; my fight alfo was confiderably

fiderably impaired, fo that, upon the whole, I exhibited as ftriking a picture of mifery as could poffibly be painted to the eye of imagination.

I HAD not been many minutes in the cabbin, when my people came running down, with looks of unutterable defpair, and informed me, in accents fcarce intelligible, that the veffel was making from us as faft as fhe could, and that there was nothing now left for us but inevitable deftruction. — I crawled up to the deck, at this terrible intimation, with all the expedition I was mafter of, and found, to my inexpreffible affliction, that their account was but too true. — The captain had taken the reefs out of his topfails and mainfail, and, in lefs than five hours, having a fine breeze in his favour, was entirely out of fight. — As long as my poor fellows could retain the leaft trace of him they hung about the fhrouds, or ran in a ftate of abfolute phrenzy from one part of

the

the fhip to the other, to collect ftill more
vifible fignals of diftrefs, — they pierced
the air with their cries, encreafing in their
lamentations as he leffened upon their view,
and ftraining their very eye-balls to pre-
ferve him in fight, through a defpairing
hope that fome dawning impulfe of pity
would yet induce him to commiferate our
fituation, and lead him to ftretch out the
bleffed hand of relief. — But, alas! to
what purpofe did we exhauft our little
ftrength in fupplicating for compaffion,
or aggravate our own misfortunes with a
fruitlefs expectation of fuch a change. —
The inexorable captain purfued his courfe
without regarding us, and fteel'd, as he un-
doubtedly muft be, to every fentiment of
nature and humanity, poffibly, valued himfelf not a little upon his dexterity in cafting us off. — Notwithftanding I muft feel
an everlafting indignation againft this bar-
barous man, for flattering people in our
circumftances, with promifes which he ne-
never meant to fulfil, I fhall not hang him

up

up to univerfal deteftation or infamy, by communicating his name to the reader;— if he is capable of reflexion his own confcience muft fufficiently avenge my caufe; and God grant that the pungency of that confcience may be my only avenger. — One inftance of his cruelty I muft not forbear to mention.—At our firft meeting I told him, neither I nor any of my men would defire a fingle morfel of his provifions, provided he only took us out of our own wreck, in which we were every moment expofed to the mercy of the waves, as our leaks were continually encreafing, and the men declining in their ftrength in proportion as the neceffity grew urgent to employ them at the pumps. — This requeft he abfolutely refufed; though the indulgence of it might, in any fucceeding diftrefs, have done him an effential fervice, and could not poffibly expofe him to the leaft inconvenience.

My

My people being thus unhappily cut off from all affiftance, where they were fo fully perfuaded of meeting with an inftant relief, became now as much dejected with their difappointment as they grew former-ly tranfported with their joy. — A defpe-rate kind of gloom fat upon every face, which feemed regardlefs of the horror that was continually expected to burft upon our heads, at the fame time that it indicated a determination to put off the fatal moment to the utmoft verge of poffibility : ac-tuated, therefore, by a refolution of hold-ing out as long as we were able, we turned our thoughts upon a pair of pigeons and a cat, which we had not yet deftroyed, and which were the only living animals on board befides ourfelves. — The pigeons we killed for our Chriftmas dinner, and the day following made away with our cat, cafting lots for the feveral parts of the poor creature, as there were no lefs than nine of us to partake of the repaft. — The
head

head fell to my fhare, and, in all my days,
I never feafted on any thing which appeared fo delicious to my appetite, — the
piercing fharpnefs of neceffity had entirely conquered my averfion to fuch food ;
and the rage of an incredible hunger rendered that an exquifite regale, which, on any
other occafion, I muft have loathed with
the moft infuperable difguft. — After the
çat was entirely confumed, my people began to fcrape the barnicles from the fhip's
bottom ; but the relief afforded from this
expedient was extremely trivial, as the
waves had beaten off the greateft number
that were above water, and the men were
infinitely too weak to hang over the fhip's
fide to gather them ; their continued intoxication, however, feemed, in fome meafure, to keep up their fpirits, though it
haftened the deftruction of their health,
and every dawn of reflexion was carried
off in a ftorm of blafphemy and exe-
çration.

D

For my own part I imbibed the ſtrongeſt averſion imaginable to wine; the complicated diſorders under which I laboured induced me to abſtain from it at firſt, and, as the men were perpetually heating it in the ſteerage the ſmell of it became offenſive to the laſt degree ; ſo that I ſubſiſted entirely on the dirty water which they had forſaken, half a pint of which, together with a few drops of Turlington's balſam being my whole allowance for four and twenty hours. — In this ſituation I patiently expected that deſtiny which I thought it utterly impoſſibly to avoid; and had it not been for the pangs which I felt on account of my wife and family, I ſhould have longed for the moment of diſſolution, and rejoiced at the approach of that awful period which was to put an end to all my misfortunes.

When the reader comes to conſider our total want of neceſſaries, that my

veſſel had been for ſome time leaky, that
I myſelf was emaciated with ſickneſs,
and had but one ſail in the world to di-
rect her; when he conſiders that the men
were either too weak, or too much in-
toxicated to pay a neceſſary attention to
the pump; when he likewiſe conſiders
the ſeverity of the ſeaſon, that it blew
" *black December*," as Shakeſpeare phraſes
it, and is told that we had not an inch of
candle, nor a morſel of fluſh to make any,
having long ſince eaten up every appearance of either which could be found ;
when the reader comes to conſider all
theſe things, and is, moreover, informed, that the general diſtreſs had deprived me of all command on board my
own ſhip, he will ſcarcely ſuppoſe that I
could ſuſtain any new misfortune; — yet,
ſuch was the ſeverity of my deſtiny, that
on the 28th of December (being then dri-
ven as far to the northward, by a ſeries of
ſoutherly winds, as 41 or 42 North Latitude) I was overtaken by a moſt dreadful

ſtorm

storm at N. W. by N. and N. W. and had my only remaining bit of canvaſs, the main-ſail, torn entirely away, ſo that I was now become a wreck in the fulleſt ſenſe of the expreſſion, — and death became ſo ſeemingly unavoidable, that I even gave up hope, that laſt conſolation of all the wretched, and prepared for an immediate launch into the dreadful gulph of eternity. Providence, however, thought proper to diſpoſe of me otherwiſe; and everlaſting thanks to it's infinite mercy, I am ſtill alive to labour for the advancement of my little family.

To this period of my relation I have been able to proceed circumſtantially from a reference to my journal. — The remainder, as I grew from this time utterly unable to hold a pen, muſt be collected from my memory, and from memorandums which I made at intervals with chalk, of the moſt remarkable occurrences. — The reader will recollect, that the laſt morſel of meat that we taſted

was

was our cat on the 26th of December. —
On the 13th of January following, being ftill toffed about at the difcretion of
the fea and wind, — my mate, at the
head of all the people, came to me in
the cabbin, half drunk indeed, but with
looks fo full of horror, as partly indicated
the nature of their dreadful purpofe, and
informed me, " that they could hold out
" no longer, — that their tobacco was en-
" tirely exhaufted; that they had eaten
" up all the leather belonging to the pump,
" — and even the buttons off their jackets,
" that now they had no chance in nature
" but to caft lots, and to facrifice one of
" themfelves for the prefervation of the
" reft, they therefore expected my con-
" currence to the meafure, and defired me
" to favour them with an immediate de-
" termination."

PERCEIVING them in liquor I endeavoured to footh them from their purpofe as
well as I could; begged they would retire

to

to reft, and that in cafe Providence did not interpofe in their favour by the next morning we would confult farther on the fubject. — Inftead of regarding my requeft, however, they fwore, with a determined horror of execration, that what was to be done, muft be done immediately; and that it was indifferent to them whether I acquiefed or not; for although they had been fo kind as to acquaint me with their refolution, they would oblige me to take my chance as well as another man, fince the general misfortune had levelled all diftinction of perfons.

As I had long expected fome violence to myfelf, from the exceffes of their intoxication, I had, for fome time, taken to my arms, to prevent a furprize; — but, alas! this was an idle precaution, as I was by no means able to repel force by force: — finding them, therefore, ftill deaf to my remonftrances, I told them they might purfue their own courfe, but that

that I would on no account either give orders for the death of the perfon on whom the lot might fall, nor partake, by any means, of fo fhocking a repaft. — To this they anfwered, that they would not afk my confent to flaughter the victim; and, as to eating or not eating, I might juft follow the biafs of my own inclination. — So faying they left me, and went into the fteerage, — but in a few minutes came back, informing me, that they had each taken a chance for their lives, and that the lot had fallen on a negro, who was part of my cargo. — The little time taken to caft the lot, and the private manner of conducting the decifion, gave me fome ftrong fufpicions that the poor Ethiopian was not altogether treated fairly; — but, on recollection, I almoft wondered that they had given him even the appearance of an equal chance with themfelves.—The miferable Black, however, well-knowing his fate was at hand, and feeing one of the fellows loading a

piftol

piſtol to diſpatch him, ran to me begging
I would endeavour to ſave his life. —Unfortunately for him I was totally without
power. — They therefore dragged him
into the ſteerage, where, in leſs than two
minutes, they ſhot him through the head.
— They ſuffered him to lye but a very little time before they ripped him open, in-
tending to fry his entrails for ſupper, there
being a large fire made ready for the purpoſe; — but one of the foremaſt-men,
whoſe name was James Campbell, being
ravenouſly impatient for food, tore the
liver from the body, and devoured it raw
as it was, notwithſtanding the fire at his
hand where it could be immediately dreſſ-
ed. — The unhappy man paid dear for
ſuch an extravagant impatience, for in
three days after de died raving mad, and
was, the morning of his death, thrown
overboard, — the ſurvivors, greatly as they
wiſhed to preſerve his body, being fearful
of ſharing his fate, if they ventured to
make

make as free with him, as with the unfortunate negro. — But to return,

THE black affording my people a luxurious banquet, they were bufy the principal part of the night in feafting on him, and did not retire to reft till two in the morning. — About eight o'clock next day, the mate came to afk my orders, relative to the pickling the body, an inftance of brutality which fhocked me fo much, that I grafped a piftol, and muftering all the ftrength I was mafter of, I fwore unlefs he inftantly quitted the cabbin, I would fend him after the negro. — Seeing me determined, he withdrew, — but muttered, as he went out, that the provifion fhould be taken care of without my advice, and that he was forry he had applied to me, fince I was no longer confidered as mafter of the fhip. — Accordingly he called a council, where it was unanimoufly agreed, to cut the body into

E   fmall

ſmall pieces, and to pickle it; after chopping off the head and fingers, which they threw overboard, by common conſent.

THREE or four days after, as they were ſtewing and frying ſome ſtakes, as they called the ſlices which they cut from the poor negro (for they ſtewed theſe ſlices firſt in wine, and afterwards either fryed or broiled them, I could hear them) ſay, " Damn him, though " he would not conſent to our having " any meat, let us give him ſome ;" and immediately one of them came into the cabbin, and offered me a ſtake. — I refuſed the tender with indignation, and deſired the perſon who brought it, at his peril to make the offer a ſecond time. — In fact the conſtant expectation of death, joined to the miſerable ſtate to which I was reduced, through ſickneſs and fatigue, to ſay nothing of my horror at the food with which I was preſented, entirely

entirely took away my defire of eating. — Add alfo to this, that the ftench of their ftewing and frying, threw me into an abfolute fever, and that this fever was aggravated by a ftrong fcurvy and a violent fwellng in my legs.—Sinking under fuch an accumulated load of afflictions, and being, moreover, fearful, if I clofed my eyes, that they would furprize and murder me for their next fupply, it is no wonder that I loft all relifh for fuftenance. — In reality, it would have been wonderful, had I preferved the leaft, and therefore my abftinence is not altogether fo meritorius a circumftance.

NOTWITHSTANDING the exceffes into which my people ran, they neverthe lefs hufbanded the negro's carcafe with the fevereft œconomy, and ftinted themfelves to an allowance which made it laft for many days. — But when it was nearly expended, I could hear them

frequently

frequently confulting among one another, on the moft expedient courfe to provide another fupply. — The refult of all thefe determinations, was to deftroy me, before they ran any rifque of deftroying them-felves. — The reader will naturally fup-pofe, that if I flept little before I received any pofitive knowledge of their inten-tion, I flept ftill lefs, when I became acquainted with their defigns. — In pro-portion as the negro grew lefs, fo in pro-portion my apprehenfions were encreafed, and every meal which they fat down to, I confidered as a frefh approach to deftruction.

In this manner matters went on, till the 28th or 29th of January, — when the mate, with more generofity than I could well expect, from the nature of their late private confultations, came to me again at the head of the people, faving, that the negro had for fome days been entirely eaten up, and as no

veffel

veſſel had yet appeared, to give us the
moſt diſtant glimmer of relief, there
was a neceſſity for caſting lots again ; —
ſince it was better to die ſeparately than
all at once. — They alſo told me that
they did not doubt but what I was now
hungry, and would of courſe take my
chance with them, as I had before done,
when my ſituation was infinitly leſs
deſperate. — I again attempted to argue
with them, and obſerved that the poor
negro's death had done them no ſervice,
as they were as greedy and as emaciated
as ever. — I therefore adviced them to
ſubmit to the diſpenſations of Providence
with temper, and offered to pray with
them for an immediate relief, or an
immediate eternity. — The anſwer which
they gave to this, was, that they were
now hungry, and muſt have ſomething
to eat ; and therefore it was no time to
pray ; and if I did not inſtantly conſent
to caſt lots, they would inſtantly proceed
without me.

FINDING

FINDING them thus inflexible, and having but too much reafon to fufpect fome foul proceedings unlefs I became a principal agent in the affair, I made a fhift to rife up in my bed, ordered pen, ink, and paper, and called them all into the cabbin. — There were feven of us now left; and the lots were drawn in the fame manner as the tickets are drawn for a lottery at Guildhall. — The lot, indeed, did not fall on me, but it fell on one David Flatt, a foremaftman, the only man in the fhip on whom I could place any certain dependance. — The fhock of the decifion was great; and the preparations for execution were dreadful. — The fire already blazed in the fteerage, and every thing was prepared for facrificing the wretched victim immediately. — A profound filence for fome time took poffeffion of the whole company, and would poffibly have continued longer had not the unhappy victim himfelf, who appeared

quite

quite refigned, delivered himfelf to the following effect: — " My dear friends, " meffmates, and fellow fufferers, all I " have to beg of you is to difpatch me as " foon as you did the negro, and to put " me to as little torture as you can :" then turning to one James Doud (the man who fhot the negro) " It is my defire, fays " he, that you fhould fhoot me." -- Doud readily, yet reluctantly, affented. — The unhappy victim then begged a fmall time to prepare himfelf for death : — to which his companions very chearfully agreed, and even feemed at firft unwilling to in-fift upon his forfeit life, as he was greatly refpected by the whole fhip's company. — A few draughts of wine, however, foon fuppreffed thefe dawnings of humanity ; neverthelefs, to fhew their regard, they confented to let him live till eleven the next morning, in hopes that the Divine goodnefs would, in the mean time, raife up fome other fource of relief ; — at the fame time they begged of me to read

prayers,

prayers, promifing to join me with the utmoft fervency. -- I was greatly pleafed with
this motion, —— and though but little able
to go through a tafk of that kind, I ex-
erted all my ftrength, and had the fatisfaction to obferve, that they behaved with
tollerable decency.

FATIGUED with reading fo much, I
lay down almoft ready to faint, yet could
hear the whole fhip's company talking to
the wretched Flatt; hoping that the Deity
would interpofe for his prefervation ; and
affuring him, though they never yet could
catch or even fee a fifh, they would at day-
break put out all their hooks again to try
if any thing could be caught to mitigate
their diftreffes, or to avert the feverity of
his fentence. —— Unhappily, however, the
poor fellow, unable to ftand the fhock of
his deftiny, grew aftonifhingly deaf by
midnight, and was quite delirious by four
in the morning. —— His meffmates difco-
vering this alteration, debated whether it
would

would not be an act of humanity to difpatch him immediately : — but the firft
refolution [to fpare him till eleven, vifibly
preponderating, they all retired to reft,
except the perfon who was to take care of
the fire. In all their exceffes they were
fenfible of what importance it was to pre-
ferve the fire, and therefore never went
to bed without leaving a centinel to keep
it up.

About eight o'clock the next morning,
as I was ruminating in my cabbin on the
approaching fate of the poor fellow, who
had now but three hours to live, two of
my people came haftily down, with looks
full of the ftrongeft expectation, and feiz-
ing my hands, without faying a fyllable,
gave me no little apprehenfion that they intended to poftpone his fate for fome time,
and to facrifice me in his ftead: — I was
the more confirmed in this opinion, as the
unhappy man ftill continued out of his
fenfes, and on that account might be judg-

F   ed

ed improper fuſtenance ; eſpecially as notwithſtanding all their neceſſities, they
threw Campbell overboard through a fear
of catching his infection. — Fraught with
a notion of this nature, I diſengaged myſelf as well as I was able, and ſnatching up
one of my piſtols, reſolved to ſell my life
as dearly as I could. — The poor men,
gueſſing at my miſtake, with ſome difficulty told me, that their behaviour was
not the effect of any ill intention, but the
actual conſequence of their joy, — that
they had deſcried a ſail to the leeward,
which appeared to be a large veſſel, and that
ſhe ſeemed to ſtand for us in as fair a direction as we could poſſibly wiſh. — The
reſt of the crew came down immediately
after their companions, and confirmed the
report of a ſail, but with this material
difference, that ſhe ſeemed to bear off upon quite a contrary courſe.

IT is impoſſible to deſcribe the exceſs of
my tranſport upon hearing that there was
a ſail at any rate in ſight — my joy, in a
manner,

manner, overpowered me ; and it was not without the utmoſt exertion of my ſtrength that I deſired them to uſe every expedition in making a ſignal of diſtreſs. — Our veſſel, indeed, itſelf was a moſt ſtriking ſignal ; but as there was a poſſibility for the ſhip in view to ſuppoſe that there was not a living creature on board, I judged it abſolutely expedient to prevent the likelihood of ſo dreadful a miſtake. — My poor men found my orders now ſo eſſential to their own preſervation, that I was obeyed with all imaginable alacrity, and had frequently the inexpreſſible happineſs to hear them jumping on the deck, and crying out, " ſhe nighs us ; ſhe nighs " us ; ſhe is ſtanding this way." — The ſhip coming viſibly nearer and nearer, my people now began to think of their unfortunate meſſmate Flatt, who was, however, utterly unable to receive any account of the deliverance which was ſo happily at hand : — nevertheleſs, in the midſt of all their ſympathy for his ſituation, they pro-

poſed

pofed a can of joy; — and it was with the greateft difficulty that I could prevail on them to acknowledge the ftrong impropriety of fuch a motion in their prefent circumftances. — I obferved that if they appeared any way difguifed with liquor the fhip might probably decline to take us on board ; and endeavoured to convince them that their deliverance in a very great meafure depended upon the regularity of this moment's behaviour. — My remonftrances had fome effect, — and all but my mate, who had for a confiderable time abandoned himfelf to a brutality of intoxication, very prudently poftponed fo untimely an inftance of indulgence.

AFTER continuing for a confiderable time, eagerly obferving the progrefs of the veffel, and undergoing the moft tumultuous agitation that could be created by fo trying a fufpence, we had at laft, the happinefs to fee a boat drop aftern, and row towards us full manned, with a very vigorous

rous difpatch. — It was now quite calm, yet, the impatience with which we expected the arrival of the boat was incredible; the numberlefs difappointments we had met in the courfe of our unfortunate voyage, filled us with an apprehenfion of fome new accident that might fruftrate all our hopes, and plunge us again into an aggravated diftrefs. — Life and death feemed, in fhort, to fit upon every ftroke of the oar ; and as we ftill confidered ourfelves tottering on the very verge of eternity, the conflict between our wifhes and our fears may be eafily fuppofed by a reader of imagination.—The boat, at length, came along-fide : but our appearance was fo ghaftly that the men refted upon their oars, and, with looks of inconceivable aftonifhment, demanded what we were. — Having fatisfied them in this point, they immediately came on board, and begged we would ufe the utmoft expedition in quitting our miferable wreck, left they fhould be overtaken by any gale before
they

they were able to recover their ship ; — at the fame time feeing me totally incapable of getting into the boat without affiftance, they provided ropes, by which I was quickly let down, and my people followed me, I need not, I believe, obferve, with all the alacrity they poffeffed.

WE were now juft preparing to fet off, when one of my people cried out that the mate was ftill on board. — In the general hurry every man's attention was engaged by the thought of his own prefervation, and it was almoft a matter of wonder that any body remembered the abfence of the mate. — He was, however, immediately called to, and, after fome time, came to the gunnel, in a feeming aftonifhment, at fuch a number of people, the can of joy, with which he had been bufy, having completely erafed every idea of the preceding occurrences from his recollection. — Having got him into the boat, we inftantly put off, and in about an hour came up to the ſhip, which was rather better than two miles from our wreck, and we were received with a humanity on board, that did the higheſt honour imaginable to the character of the captain. — When we came along ſide, he, together with his paſſengers and people, were upon deck, from an equal mixture of compaſſion and curioſi- ty, — but our hollow eyes, ſhrivelled cheeks, long beards, and ſquallid com- plexions, had ſuch an effect upon them, that the captain himſelf abſolutely ſhook with horror, as he was politely leading me to his cabbin, and generouſly thank- ing God for being made the inſtrument of my deliverance.

BEFORE I proceed farther, it is neceſſary to inform the reader of the perſon to whoſe benignity my people and I were indebted for our preſervation. — His name is THOMAS EVERS, — he commands the ſhip Suſanna, in the
Virginia

Virginia trade, and was now returning
from VIRGINIA to LONDON ; to the
latter of which places his veſſel belongs.

I HAD no ſooner got on board the
Suſanna, than dropping on my knees
againſt a hencoop on the deck, I poured
out my ſoul in a ſtrain of the ſincereſt
gratitude to the great Author of all things
for the abundance of his mercy, and in
the fulneſs of my heart began alſo to ex-
preſs my ſenſibility to the captain for his
readineſs to aſſiſt the diſtreſſed ; but it was
much eaſier for the generous EVERS to
perform fifty good actions, than to hear
the juſt applauſe of one. — He begged
I would be ſilent on the ſubject, at leaſt
for that time, — adviſed me to take a little reſt, and promiſed, if the weather
proved any way moderate, he would lye
by my wreck the whole night, and try if
there was not a poſſibility to ſave ſome of
my cloaths, aſſuring me at the ſame time,
that my people ſhould be treated with every neceſſary attention.

I WAS

I was now on board for three or four days when I found fome little inclination to eat: — the reft which I had taken during that interval giving me fome diftant dawnings of an appetite, I therefore hinted my defire to the captain, who had repeatedly applied to me from my firft arrival to take a little food, and he immediately ordered fome fego to be dreffed, of which I ate, without finding any relifh whatever, my tafte being rendered infenfible, as I apprehend, from fo long a difcontinuance of fuftenance. — Next day I had a little chicken broth, which agreed tolerably well with the weaknefs of my ftomach ; — but having an occafion for a particular indulgence of nature, I thought I fhould have expired in performing it, — the pain it gave me was excruciating to the laft degree, and the parts were fo contracted having never been once employed for a fpace of thirty-fix or thirty feven days, that I almoft began to defpair re-

G

ftoring

ftoring them to their neceffary operations.
— I was, however, at laft relieved by the
difcharge of a callous lump about the fize
of a hen's egg, and enjoyed a tranquility
of body, notwithftanding all my diforders,
with which I was utterly unacquainted for
fome preceding weeks.

THE undeviating tendernefs which my
worthy friend, the captain, fhewed to
every thing which concerned my cafe, or
tended to the recovery of my health, in
a fhort time made me able to crawl upon
deck by myfelf, though at firft I could by
no means face the wind : — the air, however, did me incredible fervice, and I continued daily increafing in my ftrength when
a frefhcalamity feemed ready to involve us,
and threatened not only to fall upon my
people and myfelf, but, in fome meafure,
through our means, upon the worthy captain EVERS, his paffengers, and fhip's
company. — The Sufanna, it feems, a
few days before fhe took me up, had been
attacked by a hard gale of wind, in which,

shipping a heavy sea, they loft four hogs, four or five hogsheads of fresh water, forty or fifty head of fowls, and twenty or thirty geese and turkies : — she had also loft her caboose and copper, and, in short, had suffered not a little, although, to the infinite credit of her commander, these misfortunes did not occasion the leaft diminution of his humanity, when he was called to by the voice of diftrefs. — Thefe loffes, together with the unexpected addition of feven perfons, and a long feries of very bad weather, obliged the captain to fet all hands to an allowance, which was eftablished at two pounds and a half of bread per week, a quart of water, and half a pound of falt provifions, a day for each man on board. — In this fituation, with a head wind, and the pumps continually at work, his ship being very leakey, we began to keep as good a look out as poffible in hopes of meeting with fome veffel which might oblige us with a falutary fupply of provifions. — No veffel, however, encountered

us,

us, but a Frenchman from Cape FRAN-
COIS, who ſtood as much in want of
neceſſaries as ourſelves. — Nevertheleſs,
about the firſt or ſecond of March we
happily reached the LAND's END, and
took in a pilot, who hailed us off DART-
MOUTH, came on board, and carried the
ſhip into that harbour: — there the captain
and the paſſengers went on ſhore, and gave
me a moſt cordial congratulation on my arrival. One circumſtance I had almoſt forgot; though it was to me a very material
one. — After I had gained a little ſtrength
on board the Suſanna, I thought I might
meſs in common with the captain and paſſengers, but indulging myſelf rather too
freely on a roaſted turkey, it threw me into
a fever; at which the good-natured captain
was ſo much affected, that he took upon
himſelf the office both of phyſician and
nurſe, and kept me under a proper reſtraint
in my food during the remainder of our
voyage.

THE

THE next day my inconfiderate mate, Mr. Archibald Nicolfon, who had fo long wallowed, as I may fay, in every mire of excefs, having reduced himfelf, by a continued intoxication, to fuch a ftate, that no proper fuftenance would ftay on his ftomach, fell a martyr to his inebriety; having a watch and fome trinkets about him, which defrayed the expence of his funeral, he was decently interred. — As to the reft of my people, the unhappy Flatt ftill continued out of his fenfes, and there were but two of the whole fix in a condition to do any duty from the time of our being taken up by captain EVERS till our arrival at DARTMOUTH.

WHILE we lay here the governor, Mr. ARTHUR HOLDSWORTH, treated me with remarkable civility, fending Mr. Stapleton, his fecretary, on board with a defire of feeing me. — I immediately accepted of his polite invitation, and, after dinner, he ge-
neroufly

neroufly offered to furnifh me with money,
or any thing I might want for my journey
to LONDON. -- The worthy captain EVERS
had rendered every affiftance of this nature
unneceffary, fo that I declined his offer
with a proper acknowledgment. — Captain EVERS having by this time fent in a
proper fupply of provifions, we fet fail for
the DOWNS that evening. — On our arrival here the captain, who was a RAMS-
GATE man, and had feveral near relations
at that place, took me afhore with him,
on a vifit to his friends, who received me
with every mark of good-nature and cordi-
ality. — We ftaid at RAMSGATE two
days, and then took a poft-chaife to MAR-
GATE ROADS, with an intent of meeting
the fhip ; but the pilot, having a frefh
wind, had taken her by ; on which we proceeded to CANTERBURY, where we lay
that night, and the next morning fet out in
the machine for LONDON.

As

As I had infured at NEW-YORK I thought it neceſſary, for the intereſt of my owners, to lodge a Proteſt for their indemnity. — Accordingly, on my arrival at LONDON I had recourſe to a Notary Public for that purpoſe, and have here inſerted the papers and atteſtations which were conſequently drawn up, as a proof of the principal circumſtances which I have mentioned in the foregoing narrative. — I am now returning to NEW-YORK, in the ſhip Hope, captain BENJAMIN DAVIS ; where I ſhortly hope the goodneſs which I have already experienced at the hand of Providence will be crowned by a joyful meeting of my wife and family.

COPIA.

C O P I A.

BY THIS PUBLIC INSTRUMENT of Declaration and Proteſt, Be it known and manifeſted unto all thoſe who ſhall ſee theſe preſents, or hear the ſame read, That on this day, the firſt of April, One thouſand, ſeven hundred, and ſixty-ſix, before me Robert Shank, Notary and Tabellion, public dwelling in LONDON, by Royal Authority, duly admitted and ſworn, perſonally appeared Mr. DAVID HARRISON, late maſter of the good ſloop or veſſel, called the Peggy, who declared, That being with his ſaid ſloop, at FYAL, loaden with wines, brandy, and one negro ſlave or black man, he ſet ſail from thence the twenty-fourth day of October now laſt paſt, bound for NEW-YORK, that in proſecution of his ſaid voyage, on the fourth of November following, being in the latitude of 38 d. 2 m. and longitude 52 d. 3 m. Weſt from

from LONDON, he was overtaken with a violent hard gale of wind at North Weſt, which ſplit the mainſail, under which ſhe was lying too, and obliged him to bend a ſpare one he had then on board: That on the ſixth following, by the violence of another hard gale of wind, two ſhrouds of each ſide his maſt were carried away, which cauſed the appearer to get up two runners and tackles for the ſupport of the maſt: That on the ſix-teenth following, in latitude of 39 d. 41 m. North and longitude 55 d. 13 m. Weſt from LONDON, there came on terrible hard gales of wind from the South South-Eaſt, attended with a large ſea, by means whereof the ſquare ſail head was carried away and tore to pieces, and obliged the appearer to heave too under a ballanced main-ſail; and notwithſtanding the jib was well ſecured on the bowſprit with points, ſtill, by the violence of the wind, they all blew up, and the ſail was ſhattered to pieces: That on the firſt of December

alſo

alfo following, in the latitude of 40 d. 1 m. North, and longitude 58 d. 37 m. Weft from LONDON, he was again overtaken with other violent hard gales of wind at Weft North Weft, with a large growing fea, which broke two of the main chain-plates, fplit the fore-fail all to pieces, and by the floop's labouring and ftraining, caufed her to be very leakey, and obliged the appearer to lay her too under a ballanced main-fail : That on the twenty-eighth of the fame month, after having met with fundry hard gales of wind from the Weft by North, to the North-Weft, he came into the latitude of 42 d. 5 m. North, and longitude 62 d. 43 m. Weft from LONDON, the wind came on to blow very terrible at North-Weft and by North, and the fea very turbulent, his floop became very leakey, and the violence of the wind increafing, the main-fail (being the only fail he had then left) was blown from the boom and gaff, and the provifions of all forts being entirely exhaufted, the

floop

floop became a perfect wreck, toſſed about at the mercy of the winds and weather, and the appearer and his crew periſhing for want of the neceſſaries of life: That on or about the thirteenth of January following, after having kept conſtantly pumping, the floop being very leakey, poſſeſſed of no kind of ſail to ſpread, and enable him to make for any port whatſoever, himſelf and crew ſtarving, and no kind of aſſiſtance appearing, they (that is to ſay) the crew, came to a reſolution, rather than all ſhould periſh for want of ſubſiſtance, to caſt lots for one to die amongſt them, to ſupport the reſt; and, in purſuance of ſuch their reſolution, intimated to this appearer, that he muſt bear his lot amongſt them; and preſently after (as this appearer was informed, he being ill in his cabbin) the lot fell upon the negro ſlave or black man, which had been part of his cargo out from NEW-YORK, and was returning there, not having been ſold at FYAL,

who

who, in a fhort time, was killed, and his faid crew fed upon him for feveral days afterwards: And, on the twenty-ninth following, being almoft famifhed, they refolved to kill another among the floop's company, to endeavour to fupport themfelves, untill the Almighty fhould bring fome veffel to their relief, and intimated fuch their refolution to the appearer for him to bear his lot amongft them, which having drawn, the melancholy chance fell on David Flatt, a feaman on board, whom they required to prepare for death by eleven o'clock the next day: But the next morning he became deaf and infenfible, and previous to that appointed hour, to wit, about nine o'clock in the forenoon, of the thirtieth of January laft, of the prefent year, one thoufand feven hundred and fixty-fix, they perceived a fail, the captain whereof humanely came towards them in the latitude of 39 d. 24 m. North, and longitude 45 d. 24 m. Weft from LONDON, but

but the wind falling calm he fent his boat
on board to fee if any one was living,
when the appearer, and the remainder of
his crew, being feven perfons in all (ex-
clufive of the fad black who had been
killed, and one JAMES CAMBELL, a feaman, who died in three days after eating
part of the faid black's liver raw) were
carried in her on board the faid fhip, which
appeared to be the Sufanna, captain THO-
MAS EVERS, bound from VIRGINIA to
LONDON, who received them very kind-
ly on board; but as this appearer's faid
floop Peggy was an intire wreck, very
leakey, and deftitute of provifions, yards,
fails and ftanding rigging (having only one
fhroud of each fide the maft left) fo that
there was no poffibility of faving her and her
cargo, they intirely quitted her, and the
wind came on to blow very hard the following night, according to all probability, fhe,
together with her cargo, muft have gone to
the bottom, and been totally loft: That the
appearer, and the refidue of his faid floop's

crew continued on board the faid fhip Sufanna in her then intended further profecution of her voyage ; in the courfe
whereof, by means of the great fatigue
they had fuftained, and the hardfhips they
had undergone, three of his faid floop's
crew, to wit, Archibald Nicolfon, mate,
and James Doud, and John Warner, fea-
men, died in the paffage, fo that there
only remained the appearer himfelf, Le-
muel Afhley, Samuel Wentworth, and the
before-mentioned David Flatt, who arrived
alive ; and now, upon his, the appearer's
firft arrival here, he, for his own juftifica-
tion, declared to proteft, as by thefe prefents
I, the faid Notary, at his requeft do hereby
folemnly proteft, that all damage, lofs, de-
triment, and prejudice, that fhall, or may
have happened, for, or by reafon or means
of the total lofs of his before-mentioned
floop Peggy and her cargo ; or the kill-
ing of the before-mentioned negro flave,
or black man, who compofed a part of her
cargo, is, and ought to be, borne by the
merchants,

merchants, freighters, and others interest-
ed therein ; the fame having accrued in
manner herein before particularly fet forth,
and not by or through any neglect, de-
fault, concurrence, direction, or mifma-
nagement of him, the appearer, or any of
his mariners, who feverally did, to the
utmoft of their power, for the prefervation of the faid floop and her cargo ; nor
was it by or through any other reafon or
motive, that his faid crew killed the before-mentioned negro, than dire neceffity,
and to prevent the reft of them from pe-
rifhing through hunger and want, after
the whole of the provifions were expended, through a long and tedious paffage, oc-
cafioned by the tempeftuoufnefs of the
winds and weather, which had deprived the
appearer of every means poffible, even to
attempt to put into any port or place whatfo-
ever for relief, although, at the time of her
departure from FYAL aforefaid, fhe was
tight, ftaunch, and ftrong, and had her
hatches well and fufficiently fecured, her
cargo

cargo well flowed, and being manned,
provided, and properly furnifhed with provifions, ftores, and neceffary appurtenances,
fhe thereby became fea-worthy, and, in
all refpects, fitted and completed, for fuch
a floop and voyage, whereof an act being
required of me the faid Notary, I have
granted thefe prefents under my Notarial
Firm and Seal of Office, to ferve and avail
where needful. Thus done and paffed in
LONDON aforefaid, in the prefence of the
under-written witneffes.

Witneffes,   DAVID HARRISON.
WM. CROFTS,   In Teftimonium veritatis
DAVID ELIAS,   ROB. SHANK, Not. Pub.

(L. S.)   1766.

DAVID HARRISON, late com-
mander of the good floop or veffel
called the PEGGY, and THOMAS EVERS,
commander of the good fhip or veffel
called the Sufannah, jointly, and feverally,
make

make oath, and JOHN WHINNEY, late a paffenger on board the faid fhip Sufanna, being one of the people called Quakers, folemnly affirmeth as follows, to wit, and firft the faid DAVID HARRISON, for himfelf depofes and fays, that the contents of the aforegoing Declaration or Proteft, made and figned by him this deponent, DAVID HARRISON, is juft and true in every article thereof, as God fhall help him, this deponent. And the faid THOMAS EVERS and JOHN WHINNEY, for themfelves fay, that on the thirtieth day of January laft paft, being at fea on board the above-mentioned fhip Sufanna, in the latitude of 39 d. 24 m. North, and longitude 45 d. 24 m. Weft from LONDON, they fell in with a wreck floop, for which they made fail ; but the wind falling calm, the faid THOMAS EVERS fent his boat on board to fee if there was any one alive in her, which boat foon after returned with feven perfons in her, being the deponent, DAVID HARRISON, and fix of the crew belonging to the faid

I   wreck,

wreck, which appeared to be the floop Peggy, bound from FYAL for NEW-YORK, with a cargo of wine and brandy, having been at fea ninty-nine days, and was then without a morfel of provifions on board, without any fail to fpread, or any ftanding rigging over the maft (except one fhroud on each fide) was very leakey, and the crew fo weak as to render them incapable of pumping, or doing any duty on board, fo that fhe muft have funk in fhort time, and as the wind blew very hard the following night, according to all probability, fhe and her cargo went to the bottom and were all loft.

Sworn this 14th day of April, 1766, by the faid David Harrifon and Thomas Evers, and affirmed by the faid John Whinney, before me

GEO. NELSON, Mayor.

DAVID HARRISON.
THOMAS EVERS,
JOHN WHINNEY.

THE

THE aforegoing is a true, faithful, literal, and exact copy of it's original, paſſed
before me the under-written Notary, and
ſworn to by DAVID HARRISON and
THOMAS EVERS, and affirmed to by JOHN
WHINNEY therein named, before the
Right Hon. GEORGE NELSON, Eſq.
Lord Mayor, and one of his Majeſty's
Juſtices of the Peace for this city of LON-
DON ; and after duly examining and colating theſe preſents therewith, and finding
them ſo to agree in every particular, I at-
teſt the ſame in conformity, whereof an
act being required of me the ſaid Notary,
I have granted theſe preſents, under my
Notarial Firm and Seal of Office, to ſerve
and avail as occaſion may be or require.
Done in LONDON this 14th day of April,
1766.

ROB. SHANK, Not. Pub.

1766.

C O P I A.

DAVID HARRISON, late mafter of the good floop or veffel called the Peggy, maketh oath upon the Holy Evangelifts of Almighty God; That being with his faid floop at FYAL he there received on board her a cargo of merchandize, confifting of twenty pipes of brandy, feventy-three pipes of wine, in pipes, half pipes, and quarter cafks, and one negro flave, or black man; the cafks of brandy and wine being marked with the mark A. M. and the negro, or black, called or named Wiltfhire (and had been part of this deponent's latter cargo from NEW-YORK, for FYAL, but was returning from thence not having been there fold) with which cargo he was bound, with his faid floop, from FYAL aforefaid for NEW-YORK, and accordingly departed in the profecution of his faid voyage, on the twenty-fourth day of October laft paft, 1765;

but

but in the profecution of his faid intended voyage, on the thirtieth day of January following, and alfo laft paft, in or about the latitude of 39 d. 24 m. North, and and longitude 45 d. 24 m. Weft from LONDON, after having exhaufted all his provifions, his fails and rigging blown to pieces and gone; and his faid floop having become very leakey, this deponent, and the remainder of his crew, being feven perfons, were miraculoufly preferved and taken from on board the faid floop Peggy, on board the fhip Sufanna, whereof THOMAS EVERS was commander; and as the wind came to blow very hard the following night, his faid floop Peggy, together with her cargo, herein before enumerated; according to all probability, went to the bottom that night, and were totally loft. And this deponent further depofeth and faith, that his faid floop's cargo was fo fhipped at FYAL aforefaid, by Meffrs. Gaythorn and Graham, merchants

merchants there, who had bills of lading
for the fame, and who did fend their
papers, letters, and difpatches to this deponent, directed to Meffrs. William Malcom,
and John Alexander and company, the
confignees of the faid cargo at NEW-
YORK; and this deponent faith, that
the faid papers, letters, and difpatches
were put up by him into his own cheft;
but being taken out of his faid floop in
a very great hurry, he had not time to
take the fame thereout, fo that the faid
papers, letters, and difpatches, together
with this deponents faid cheft, and all
and fingular his own papers and appurtenances were (according to the beft of
this deponent's knowledge and belief)
totally loft in and with his faid floop
Peggy and her cargo.

Sworn this 15th day
of April, 1766, be-   DAVID HARRISON.
fore me in LONDON.

GEORGE NELSON, Mayor.

THE

THE aforegoing is a true, faithful, literal, and exact copy of it's original, sworn
by the deponent DAVID HARRISON,
before the Right Hon. GEORGE NELSON,
Esq. Lord Mayor, and one of his Ma-
jesty's Justices of the Peace for this
city of LONDON; and after duly examining and colating these presents therewith, and finding them so to agree in
every particular, I attest the same in
conformity, whereof an act being required of me the said Notary, I have
granted these presents under my Notorial
Firm and Seal of Office, to serve and
avail where needful. Done in LONDON,
this 15th day of April, 1766.

ROB. SHANK, Not. Pub.

1766.

C O P I A

C O P I A.

THIS is to certify whom it may concern, That on the Thirtieth day of January, 1766. in the latitude 39 d. 24 m. North, and in the longitude 45 d. 24 m. Weſt from LONDON, I fell in with a wreck ſloop, made ſail for her, but falling calm, ſent my boat on board in order to ſee if any body was alive; ſhe returned with ſeven perſons, being the captain and reſidue of the crew; ſhe proved to be the ſloop Peggy, DAVID HARRISON, commander, from FYAL bound to NEW-YORK, had been at ſea ninety-nine days, not a morſel of proviſions on board, not a yard of canvaſs to ſpread, and no ſtanding rigging over the maſt, having only one ſhroud of a ſide, very leakey, and the crew not being able to pump, ſhe muſt have ſunk in

a ſhort

a short time, (that next night blowing a very hard gale of wind) unless some vessel fortunately fell in with her. The cargo consisted of wine, and brandy, which was all lost with her, and nothing being saved.

Attested by us, THOMAS EVERS.
FRANCIS M'LEAN.
JOHN WHINNEY,
Passenger on board the Susanna.

THE aforegoing is a true, faithful, literal, and exact copy of it's original, granted and signed by Captain THOMAS EVERS, commander of the good ship or vessel called the Susanna ; FRANCIS M'LEAN, chief mate thereof, and JOHN WHINNEY, late a passenger in the said ship; the which said THOMAS EVERS and JOHN WHINNEY, on the day of the date hereof, personally came and appeared before me the underwritten

K   Notary,

Notary, and folemnly and fincerely declared, that the contents thereof were,
in every refpect, true. In Teftimony
whereof I have granted thefe prefents,
under my Notorial Firm and Seal of
Office, this 14th day of April, 1766.

In Teftimonium Veritatis
Rob. Shank, Not. Pub.
1766.

Copy

Copy of a LETTER from Meſſrs. GAY-
THORN and GRAHAM, Merchants in
FYAL, to Mr. WILLIAM MALCOM,
Merchant at NEW-YORK, dated Octo-
ber the 21ſt, 1765.

S I R,

WE forgot till our letters were ſealed
to make any mention of Captain
HARRISON ; this will ſerve as a certificate
of his prudent behaviour and induſtry, in
every thing that concerns the owners whilſt
here, and that if it had not been for the
ſtormy weather we have had, the good
diſpatch he gave on board, would have
got him from this place much ſooner.
We are very reſpectively,

S I R,

Your moſt obedient humble ſervants,

GAYTHORN and GRAHAM.

THE above letter was ſent me on board
the day I ſailed, and remained with me
in my pocket till the day I was taken up,
which I hope may anſwer nearly the time
I was out at ſea when taken up.

DAVID HARRISON.